Could I Have This Dance Forever?

Could I Have This Dance Forever?

SHAWNA BAIS

RESOURCE *Publications* • Eugene, Oregon

COULD I HAVE THIS DANCE FOREVER?

Copyright © 2024 Shawna Bais. All rights reserved. Except for brief quotations in critical publications or reviews, no part of this book may be reproduced in any manner without prior written permission from the publisher. Write: Permissions, Wipf and Stock Publishers, 199 W. 8th Ave., Suite 3, Eugene, OR 97401.

Resource Publications
An Imprint of Wipf and Stock Publishers
199 W. 8th Ave., Suite 3
Eugene, OR 97401

www.wipfandstock.com

PAPERBACK ISBN: 979-8-3852-1336-8
HARDCOVER ISBN: 979-8-3852-1337-5
EBOOK ISBN: 979-8-3852-1338-2

03/18/24

This is to my mother, who inspired and encouraged my poem writing and is an amazing poet herself. For my dad, whose voice still guides me. For my sister, who is the most extraordinary woman I know. For my husband, my best friend, my greatest supporter, and the love of my life. For my daughter, who fills my heart with joy each and every day. To my step-daughters, who dare to envision a better world. To my pets, who sat beside me while I wrote this. To my readers, who find a piece of themselves within these poems, may you find the courage, joy and love to live it. To my brother, who left us too soon, you will never be forgotten.

CONTENTS

Introduction	ix
A Love Deeper Than This	1
The Colt	3
A Patient So Small	4
The Brown Puppy	6
The Drink	7
Graduation	10
Mare	12
Is Anyone There?	14
Man and Car	16
Memory	18
Camping	19
Gone	20
My One and Only	22
A Friend Indeed	24
Family	26
The Exam	28
Grandpa	30
Thanksgiving	32
Newborn Puppy	33
To Hear	35
Childhood	36
The House	38
Butterfly	40
The Kitten	41
The Hawk	43

First Steps	44
Race of a Lifetime	46
Heaven	48

INTRODUCTION

Poetry is so much more than just mere words. I like poems that have a deep, meaningful theme that very few other means of communication can covey. These poems each transport me to a memory and intertwine realizations that I have had over the years. Each one is special and unique in its own right. I hope that they will be relatable to you and provoke the same depth of feelings and emotions that I felt as you journey through them. I have written these verses in hopes that they will not only entertain, but will have a lasting impact to inspire you to not only revel in the dance we call life, but to also yearn for the day when we can truly have this dance forever.

A LOVE DEEPER THAN THIS

The waves on the beach, crashed onto the sand
As a mother of two, held each with one hand

The kids jumped and giggled, what fun it would be
To play here with Mom, to have the day free

Her legs weren't thin or muscled, her thighs had a jiggle
Her arms and her stomach, had more than a wiggle

Her swimsuit was old, and her face wasn't tan
But then I looked up, as across the beach he ran

His eyes met hers, then glowed when they met
A look of pure love, of joy, not a bit of regret

His arm went around her, so proud and so free
That she looked amazing, you'd have to agree

The beauty was deeper, than the lines on her face
That he thought her perfect, full of strength and of grace

And as they walked together, smiling arm in arm
I couldn't help but admire, her grace and her charm

And the birds above, sang out with a song
As the kids danced in the waves, as they walked along

And I could hear the song, of old and of new
But one that never changes, that always is true

To love what you have, to value more than the outside
Happiness is greater, than the flaws we try to hide

And I smiled as they passed, each ones' eyes aglow
And from my lips, the song did start to flow

How I wish we all, could have this kind of treasure
Could I, could I, could I have this dance forever?

THE COLT

He's gangly and awkward and fighting to stand
He tips and sways and who knows where he'll land

His mother knickers and nuzzles his soft little head
But her words of encouragement don't have to be said

Slowly but surely more confidence he gains
He crashes at times, but ignores all the pains

Then suddenly the soft moonlight on him does shine
How gorgeous, how precious, this little foal of mine

The soft moonlight on his new coat does play
Welcoming baby to his very first day

And quickly to my lips, a whisper does come
A tune, a song, my heart starts to hum

He kicks up his heels and then runs away
This time he's steady, with barely a sway

The song beats stronger, it then breaks out
The wish from my soul, the words start to spout

In my heart I wish this moment never to sever
Oh please, could I, could I have this dance forever?

A PATIENT SO SMALL

The ventilator swooshes and the heart monitor beeps
But still my little patient, so quietly sleeps

His arms bent and crooked, with contractures so strong
Show hints of the pain, that has held him so long

His little body bent, so weak and so frail
His lips bright and rosy, yet his round face so pale

Without a sound or a cry, suddenly he wakes
Yet still on the bed, no movement he makes

His arms and legs, he can't move a bit
He can't walk or play, he can't even sit

But carefully up into my arms he will go
Then we'll start to rock, back and forth, to and fro

His warm breath on my cheek, now I will feel
Then with a soft kiss, my love will I seal

His eyes will close gently as he snuggles to me
His moment to dance, to really be free

And together we will dance, as the music does play
The disease and its chains, for a moment held at bay

Then after a time, back in his bed he will lay
But his eyes will look at me, and with them he'll say

I might not be able to move, talk or play ever
But please, please, could I have this dance forever?

THE BROWN PUPPY

His brown fur so soft, his eyes so sweet
The love I feel, I cannot repeat

He wiggles and looks up as if to say
You look like fun, why don't we play

He runs and leaps and barks with joy
A stick, a twig, he'll make it a toy

Who can beat a new puppy for fun
Is there anything better under the sun

He'll sit by your side and cry when you cry
His love and caring makes troubles pass by

Exercise with him is a fun thing to do
Whatever you ask, he'll respond to you

With this little guy I never want to part
He makes me smile and inside my heart

His devotion and love have pushed a lever
Could I, could I have this dance forever?

THE DRINK

At last the day, had finally come
Now he was a man, just turned 21

His friends all cheered and yelled hooray
Because they knew what would happen today

And to the bar, they all soon appeared
To not drink, now that would be weird

One beer, then two, they had such fun
What could be better, under the sun

The girls all smiled and looked so nice
A third beer he had, and didn't think twice

Together they left, four in all
Who was driving, I cannot recall

Around a corner, he drove so fast
What fun they cried, we're having a blast

Then into the intersection, through a red light
They couldn't be seen, because it was night

And the mother of two, who struck their car
Flew through the air, but didn't get far

And the smashing of metal, made an awful sound
As both cars tipped and spun around

And then in the stillness, they finally lay
Unaware of the price, they had yet to pay

For their friend lay, with blood on his chest
In the nearby field, where he had come to rest

The siren did wail, and the ambulance did come
Meaning medics were coming, fast on the run

They picked him up, and rushed him in
To the hospital where I, was working within

We gave him care, did the best that we could
While his mother cried, and by his side stood

And over time, as the days went past
It became clear, he just wouldn't last

She showed me pictures, of him long ago
And spoke of the past, how she watched him grow

There were pictures of him, riding a new bike
And grinning at her, after a long hike

There were pictures of him, with his very first car
And at graduation, saying he would go far

Then her sad eyes, to his still form did turn
To have him back like this, she really did yearn

To see him running and playing today
To have him be normal, to wake up and say

Mom I love you, and I always will
Be at your side, now and forever still

Her eyes pleaded, for this to be true
As the memories returned, as if they were new

Her silent wish then filled the air
Loud and clear, to all standing there

Please, oh please, don't leave me ever
Could I, could I have this dance forever?

GRADUATION

The pictures been taken, the lessons are done
School time is over, now all she wants is fun

Family and friends, all sit waiting in their seat
As the song starts to play, that old familiar beat

She straightens her cap, all ready to march
Then down the aisle she comes, smiling under the arch

Graduation has come, so quickly it seems
So many memories come back, my mind it just teems

Of her crying in my arms, that first day at home
Then starting to walk, oh how she did roam

Sleepless the nights, as I walked the floor
Listening for sounds of crying, coming through her bedroom door

Then suddenly she was off, to her first day of school
Learning math and reading, and each and every rule

The days seemed so much quieter, without her around
Where once there was laughter, now there isn't any sound

She chatted about friends, and all the fun she had
And what made her happy, and what made her sad

And how the days flew and then the years went by
Now as I watched her march, I felt myself start to cry

For while I am so proud, of the woman that she is now
I wonder if there is a way, to stop the time somehow

And have her be a child, so happy and carefree
Her braids blowing in the wind, as she swung beneath a tree

And have her in my arms, so snug and safe once more
How fast the time did go, oh why did I ignore

The little things I took for granted, in my mind they do appear
As from my eyes and down my cheek, slides a lonely tear

As I see her smile and wave, her diploma in her hand
No longer a child, today she looks so grand

And from my heart the cry does come
Then up to my lips, the tune I start to hum

I don't care who is listening, I'll sing it to whomever
Could I, could I, could I have this dance forever?

MARE

She was black and sleek, her body so strong
I'd ride her for hours, yet it never felt too long

I was just a child when she entered my life
A time of challenge, a short period of strife

She gave me stability, and the confidence to live
She stayed through it all, gave all she had to give

She was more than a horse, but a friend indeed
She fulfilled my desires, along with my need

The days turned to years and as I grew older
She was always there, when I needed a shoulder

Our rides grew fewer, but I will always know
She was first to me, even if she couldn't win a show

Then one morning so bleak and so grim
The vet came and said that her chances were slim

And as I watched that noble horse die
The memories of yesterday, seemed to pass by

The wind in my face, as we ran free
Her grace and strength, again I could see

And as my tears flowed, my heart seemed to cry
    Of a song of old, the tune seemed to fly

I saw her again, with more strength than ever
Oh please, oh please, could I have this dance forever?

IS ANYONE THERE?

The patients are too many, the nurses are too few
One is yelling about her pain, another threatens to sue

I run from room to room, trying to get things done
This headache and backache, are really just no fun

The call light is blinking, beckoning me to come
250 needs some blood, 253 just wants a tum

It all seems too much, and for a moment I wonder why
I keep being a nurse, why I even bother to try

Then from her room I see her little hand waving
She wants to tell me something, all day she's been saving

Her little old hand is soft and thin, reaching out to me
Her blue eyes look up, filled with a silent plea

She just wants to know that someone really cares
That in this cold sterile hospital, someone is still there

That in this moment of pain and doubt, she is not alone
That I am not too busy, to miss her tears and groan

That in my haste to rapidly all my duties to fulfill
To check off every duty, and hand out every pill

That I still recall the people, that I came here to care for
That I know what is more important, the person or the chore

And as I am leaving an hour late from work again
I will look in at her and I will have to grin

Because floating down the hallway, to me a song does reach
And in its words a message true, quietly it does preach

And to my tired aching body, the words push a lever
Could I, could I, could I have this dance forever?

MAN AND CAR

His eyes are closed as he waits with a smile
But his ears listen closely, hoping all the while

That soon he will hear, the roar of it start
This car he was wanting, the one of his heart

Its sleek lines and smooth paint job
Oh the look, how it makes his heart throb

To sit in the seat, become man and machine
To speed along the roadway, oh what a dream

It's no longer just an engine, and pieces of metal
It's alive and part of him, his foot on the petal

Steering wheel in hand, the wind in his hair
The worries left behind, now he doesn't care

What joy and happiness, this machine can impart
As on their journey, they rumble and dart

And as they move, as one down the road
The grin on his face, and his eyes just glowed

I could hear the song, the engine did sing
Above its roar, strong and loud it did ring

As they danced together, this man and machine
The words came to life, the song it did teem

As they left to go explore, here or wherever
Could I, could I, could I have this dance forever?

MEMORY

I arrive early, a nursing instructor starting my day
To see the nursing home, its halls in disarray

He stands by himself, holding on so he doesn't fall
He trembles as he moves, where he is he can't recall

His clothes hang loosely, his form thin and tall
The effort is taxing him, just to move down the hall

The strong smell of urine, rises up to fill the air
There are looks of sadness, wondering who is going to care

Then his eyes search out mine, the blue eyes now bright
From deep in his soul, shines forth a new light

His trembling hand reaches out, his grip now strong to feel
To grasp my hand in his, his body pulsing with new zeal

For a moment time stands still, his gaze locked tight to mine
His lips start to move, and this time his words come out fine

The urgency of his words tell me, the time is now or never
Could I, could I, could I have this dance forever?

CAMPING

The wind in the trees, the birds singing brightly
The smoke from a campfire, and the frogs croaking nightly

It's marshmallows and s'mores, and a bright yellow tent
For family and friends and another night spent

Taking a hike, in the trees and the hills
Wading in a creek, and other such thrills

Watching the dog, as she chases her ball
Then comes running back, with a whistle or call

It's buns, mayo and ketchup, and eating a crisp chip
Listening to the sizzle, as the burgers about to flip

It's crawling into a sleeping bag, after a day full of fun
And watching the stars and moon, say goodnight to the sun

It's smiling at each other, how could we be so clever
Could I, could I, could I have this dance forever?

GONE

The work day was going, lunch soon would be served
Above the bustle of activity, the phone could be heard

Then the world stopped, it all got so still
I couldn't believe my ears, it just couldn't be real

My brother, my friend, the one I adored
Had been killed while working, from a falling board

My mind went blank, and my mouth went dry
I was too much in shock, to even let out a cry

In shock I laid there, curled up in a ball
How long I laid there, I cannot recall

So many things left, so many words left unsaid
How I'd go on, the thought filled me with dread

He was strong and smart, with a family to care
A young daughter so tiny, how would she fare

But even death's grasp, the memories can't steal
I still hear his voice, and his hug I can feel

"Kiddo, you've got this, remember all those years
You spent keeping up with me, hiding all your fears

As we rode horses together, and hung out outside
Even though you were nervous, you learned how to ride

Remember the tree fort, Dad built us so tall
And how you were scared, that you might fall

But climb you did, clear up to the top
Now do the same here, don't waver or stop

And driving each day, on our way on to school
Listening to music, we thought we were so cool

My shadow you were, best friends through it all
And watch out boys, if the wrong one tried to call"

Then the memories fade, but don't disappear
Each and every one, are something I hold dear

And as we lay, your body down to rest
I will find the strength, to rise up to the test

And I know this isn't the end, though the chapter here is done
Someday I'll see you again, when earth's battle here is won

And as I sigh, and the tears run down my face
Time will pass and go, but the memories won't erase

I promise this, no matter what, I won't forget you ever
Could I, could I, could I have this dance forever?

MY ONE AND ONLY

The touch, the smile, the warmth of your embrace
How sweet it is to hold you, and look up in your face

With this ring we say our vows this day
And in front of friends and family, we bow our heads to pray

The pomp and glitter, the presents and cheers, how neat it is to see
As I remember that day last year, when you proposed on bended knee

But this is just the start of a journey, we have so far to go
There's so much more that each day, we will get to know

And I hope that each day, brings us closer than we are
Our marriage just beginning, but together we'll go far

I feel like each day, I love you more and more
You are a part of me, a part of my very core

And while I know some days, we'll argue or we'll fight
I know that when it's said and done, we'll strive to make it right

And some days won't feel, so happy and carefree
But through the good and bad, I hope that we will see

That a love like this is worth, all the work and the wait
That no matter what happens, you I won't forsake

And when one day we're old and gray and walking isn't easy
When the wrinkles come and our lungs become, oh so very wheezy

I hope you still hold my hand, and wish for one day more
And on our feet, you'll hold me tight, just like you did before

How I hope that wobbly now, to dance we'll still endeavor
And whisper softly in my ear, could I have this dance forever?

A FRIEND INDEED

His frail hand trembled as he petted his head
His face said it all, no words had to be said

His wife was gone, this was all he had left
Without his only companion, his world would be bereft

Please save him, he's all I got now
Then he looked at me, a furrow on his brow

I don't have much, I'll give all I can
Then his words faltered, and again he began

You may not understand, what this dog means to me
I wish I could explain, to help you to see

He was there by my side, when my wife took ill
And when she broke her hip, after taking a spill

I'd sit on the porch, with him by my side
He always understood, I had nothing to hide

Oh he had his hard days, as a puppy no doubt
Chewing my shoe, made me want to shout

But a friend he has been, unselfish to me
He gives all he's got, completely and free

He'd sit there and listen, when no one else would
He stayed at my side, when no one else could

The walks in the park, I remember so well
There are so many things, I could sit here and tell

I know you see lots, of other dogs here each day
But that he's my whole world, I want to convey

Our hair might be gray, and our walk not as fast
We aren't as young, and our prime is well past

But his worth is more, than the gray on his head
We just need more time, then his eyes pled

Just one more run, one more day at the park
One more long talk, and the joy of his bark

Don't let this be the end, of this journey whatsoever
Could I, could I, could I have this dance forever?

FAMILY

What is a family, I thought as I looked
At my daughter beside me, smiling as we cooked

Her arms dark and tan, her brown eyes so bright
Oh my pale skin, next to her looked so white

For who says it's just blood, for a family to make
That makes us so strong, to not separate

Born far away, in my heart she did grow
It's the love that we have, that helps us to know

That family means, being there to the end
And even on bad days, our woes we will mend

My stepdaughters two, are part of my core
Not flesh of my flesh, but still I adore

Watching them grow, their lives just beginning
Their jokes and their games, and tales they like spinning

For family is a choice, it's a love that we decide
To never give up, to stay by each other's side

Some days are hard, and we won't like each other
But we choose to forgive, and stick through whatever

To always live as all for one, and one for all
To always have your back, be there if you fall

To not point a finger, to not lay the blame
To lift each other up, and to not place the shame

The power of a family, is a reflection of our God
This family He did create, I'm thankful and I'm awed

And as I watch them play today, I'm grateful for this treasure
Could I, could I, could I have this dance forever?

THE EXAM

The house is all quiet, not one makes a peep
Yet here in the silence, I still cannot sleep

For with all my years of learning, there's one thing I know
It is only what you give, that in the end you will show

The study and the reading, the labor and the pain
Will someday be forgotten, when the prize we all do gain

And how important at this moment, that A is to me
Yet something tells me deep inside, as big as it may be

That when the stress and terror is o'er, in the middle of December
It's not the facts, or the numbers, that I will still remember

No there are more important things, that will stay in my mind
Things more precious that A's or B's, or anything else you may find

Like hiking with friends, or talking, and the laughter we do share
During class or in between, it's great to know you're there

You always listen to me, just when I need to talk
You're always steady, your friendships like a rock

Thank you for pushing me, to change and not get in a rut
To remind me to smile, and to give no matter what

I hope that I have done my part, to be a friend to you
To challenge and to make you think, about your world view

To all of you I give my thanks, but there's one I can't leave out
Because without the Lord to see me through, there really is no doubt

I wouldn't be here studying now, for these exams we have to do
And while I try to do my best, I know He'll see me through

So pass or fail, this day I know, I have been so very blessed
With friends and family, hope and joy, love and all the rest

Thanks for being there for me, the one I'll always treasure
Could I, could I, could I have this dance forever?

GRANDPA

He lay on the bed, his form still and thin
His eyes closed and silent, not a sound from within

Could this be the grandpa, I remember as a child
The one who seemed so stern, but then at me smiled

I remember thinking, he must be invincible
So strong and unerring, he stood by principle

I remember him working, every day for so long
Now he lies here sleeping, those work days all gone

He never said much, but it was always enough
He loved deeply, for a man who seemed so tough

His hands were calloused, well worn through his life
He was steadfast and faithful, 70 years with his wife

He fought in the war, and was brave as could be
So that each of his family, could always be free

He got up each day, and never complained
Finished the job, didn't stop if it rained

Men like that, seem so hard to find
Strong and true, but still oh so kind

And as I watch, my own child grow
How I wish for more time, so they could all know

The joys I have had, spending time by his side
So many memories, it's been quite a ride

How to reverse, the years now gone by
To make him so young, how I wish I could try

But as I watch him quietly, slip from our grasp
I know in my memories, he'll always last

And I hold his hand, not a child anymore
And from my lips, the words and melody tore

Please don't go, this man so strong and clever
Could I, could I, could I have this dance forever?

THANKSGIVING

The fire in the fireplace, the warmth as it burns
To be at home with family, how my heart yearns

The smell of bread baking, and the food on the table
All the family gathered round, as best as they are able

It's Thanksgiving Day, and so much to be thankful for
The laughter and the talking, oh how it makes my heart soar

Grandma and Grandpa, the respect that they do get
For grandkids all are vying, for a place close to sit

Aunts and uncles, with stories each to say
Makes this day extra special, than any other day

And at the end of this meal, so very well prepared
Pies and cakes are coming, and ice cream to be shared

The baby is laid out sleeping, the dog runs right by her
The boys are laughing loudly, and the cat softly purrs

And I have to smile, at how blessed we can be
The memories we are making, so special I can see

And how I am so thankful, to have this very treasure
Could I, could I, could I have this dance forever?

NEWBORN PUPPY

She was born one dark and stormy night, just one among them all
So dark and soft, snuggled by her mom, she looked so very small

But she was special, this little pup, with eyes that shown so bright
Her happy smile and wagging tail, could warm the darkest night

And into my heart and life she danced, her smile just all aglow
In spite of her pain and hardship, only love she did show

While I watched her adoring eyes, just follow my every move
How I wished we knew the answer, had something we could prove

Yet her smile never failed, her body waved happily as she danced
Her coat might not shimmer, but who would notice as she pranced

So happy and content with the time she had to live
How can I thank her for all the love, that she had to give

And as the days passed, and I knew the time was soon to come
In my heart I hear the song, and then the words I start to hum

And when the day came, and her body was finally laid to rest
The words broke through, the tears spilling on my breast

For once again, I could see her dance, her body now free from pain
And as she played and romped with glee, I could clearly hear the refrain

And how I wish to see her still, this precious moment to not sever
Please, oh please, could I, could I have this dance forever?

TO HEAR

The rain drops fall, with a patter on the roof
The wind whistles, a sound to give us proof

The night air is broken, by the honk of a car
Next door I can hear, the strumming of a guitar

The dog barks, and the bird sings a song
The frogs at the creek are croaking, as it trickles along

The door creaks a greeting, as it opens right now
The children's loud laughter, and the cat's soft meow

The crunch of the snow, or the rustling of the leaves
The hoot of an owl, or the force of a sneeze

How thankful I am, for this gift to be given
To know that something's there, even if it is hidden

And as I listen, for the next thing I'll hear
This much I know, for this thing is clear

A grand symphony or a bark, it's still music to me
My moment to savor, this song I will plea

That I am so thankful, that I can hear whatever
Could I, could I, could I have this dance forever?

CHILDHOOD

Today she asked with eager eyes, to tell about my past
To hear the stories of my childhood, this she brightly asked

At 3 years of age, I remember well, a new puppy we did get
And driving home I still recall, she threw up where I did sit

And riding bikes and taking hikes, with my brother after school
We rode so fast and did so great, we thought we looked so cool

And at the shop each summer day, we waded at the creek
Then built a fort and climbed a tree, each day was such a treat

My Dad would take us, on a hike each week after church
To find some treasure, I don't know what, but each time we had to search

I remember when a rattlesnake scared me, and then it made me cry
And someone laughed and my brother and sis, boldly dared ask him why

I remember how in a shoebox, our money we did save
For the dream of having a horse, our all we gladly gave

As the years pass by, the memories true, may all start to fade
But for this childhood, there is nothing, I would rather trade

I am so thankful for the years I had, and all I got to do
The fun and sad, the good and bad, how the time it just flew

And as I look at her just now, she's growing up so fast
I remind her that it may seem long, but childhood really won't last

So enjoy each moment, take the time to see
To just be a kid, to laugh and be free

For soon the years will start to pass, and age will find you too
And you will wish, for the days back then, and the things you used to do

And you'll hear the words in your head, light as a feather
Oh please, could I, could I have this dance forever?

THE HOUSE

It's just some curtains and some walls, a foundation there is laid
But the memories here that I hold dear, for these I wouldn't trade

Of playing hide and seek, every nook I did enjoy
My brother so much bigger than I, my small size I did employ

It's the smell of fresh baking bread, and dinner round the table
Its warm buns and holding hands, and soup right from the ladle

It's a warm bed with comforter soft, where I lay down each night
And my sister dear, who would always hear, if I had a fright

Its popcorn and toast, a movie to watch, together we all sit
These memories dear, of us gathered here, I never want to quit

Then on Friday, we each gathered round, and oh what music we made
With the trumpet and flute, and piano and sax, oh the music we played

The walls and the carpet, the bed and the frame, a home this does not make
It's the love and the joy, the warmth and the fun, the memories we create

As I sit here remembering, the place back then, the house now empty and cold
I wish for the days, when the house was a home, and not just memories to unfold

For the empty floors and open doors, to once again rejoice
For the ones I love, that once passed through, to again find their voice

And sing the song of old and of new, the one we sing together
Could I, could I, could I have this dance forever?

BUTTERFLY

The wings shimmer and flash, as it lands on a flower
Its beauty and grace, I could watch by the hour

Beauty I behold, the white and blue
So many butterflies, of every color and hue

Flit about in this bright field, the grass so very green
I sit here watching, mesmerized, they just have to be seen

Their life so short as they pass, but oh what joy they bring
Watching them go from flower to flower, makes me want to sing

For what small pleasure, it brings to young and old
Changing from a caterpillar, this beauty to behold

And as I watch it fly away, to find a new endeavor
Could I, could I, could I have this dance forever?

THE KITTEN

She looked to be ten, as she stood at my door,
Her eyes so worried, as she stared at the floor

The kitten she held, so weak and so pale
Its back leg all twisted, its body so frail

"I found her outside, by the road near our house
She must have been lost, or hunting a mouse

Please make her better, she's been my best friend
She sleeps on my bed, and plays without end"

A crumpled few bills, she held in her hand
As she started to cry, but continued to stand

The kitten wiggled and let out a cry
The girl's eyes pleaded, please won't you try

The story repeats, now a few weeks along
The girl bright and happy, and singing a song

The kitten is well, and climbs on her lap
Sees the string that she's holding, and gives it a tap

How pleasant to see, them both happy and well
That she is her world, you really can tell

And as I wave, and tell them goodbye
My face has a smile, my heart hears the cry

For so happy am I, as they skip down the street
This song of old, I like to repeat

How great to see, them both playful and clever
Could I, could I, could I have this dance forever?

THE HAWK

The piercing call broke through the air, as he sat there on a tree
His dark eyes bore right through my soul, and a shiver ran down me

His feathers sleek upon his back, his wings tucked at his side
Ready to spread and up he'd go, they'd take him for a ride

His talons strong to pierce a hide, yet gentle they could be
How amazing to be so close, yet know he'd soon be free

What a pleasure to have known him, if only for a time
As he spreads his wings, and then he starts to climb

How I'll miss his feisty call, but thankful for this pleasure
Oh please, could I, could I have this dance forever?

FIRST STEPS

So tiny she was, when she first came home
So eager to learn, she started to roam

At first she just crawled, around on her knees
Happy to sit, she wanted to please

Then more bold, she became with each day
She wanted to explore, to learn how to play

When she first stood alone, my how she did grin
How proud she was, to find the strength from within

Then slowly but surely a step did she take
She kept trying harder, if a stumble she'd make

My hand no longer, she wanted to hold
Each day tried harder, every day grew more bold

Until soon she was walking, and then started to prance
Then went from falling, to beginning to dance

And as I watched the time slip away
I thought of what to do, what could I say

And while I wish, a baby she'd be
I want her to grow up, to be happy and free

But as my heart lingers, on this new step she takes
A piece of me cries, and a piece of me breaks

For how I wish this moment would linger
When she would go back, and hold on my finger

But let her go, I know I must endeavor
Oh, could I, could I, could I have this dance forever?

RACE OF A LIFETIME

We went to the track, with our race car so fast
But this day was different, than had been in the past

For today we weren't racing, trying to be the fastest car
We were giving rides to kids, whose cancer had gone far

There were kids there whose legs, had been taken off one day
Their doctors trying to find an answer, to keep the cancer at bay

And one little boy with a brain tumor, he wasn't scared a bit
As the car went zooming round, so calmly he did sit

Their fears were all abated, as death they had to face
Find joy in driving round and round, so fast that they did race

Around the track they smile and cheer, their pain held at bay
Their one day to just be kids, to laugh and to play

For in their parents' eyes I see, the worry and the doubt
In their more experienced face, you know what it's about

For this might be their only ride, as death creeps ever nearer
For the tests and drugs don't always work, the picture becomes clearer

And so we smile and cheer them on, as they dance around the track
And with high fives and dancing eyes, we welcome them right back

And as they walk away, our race car sits alone
We thank the Lord for what we have, and all that we've been shown

Their smiles and laughter now drift away, but the truth is here however
Upon the breeze I hear the words, Could I, could I, could I have this dance forever?

HEAVEN

I dreamed one night, as I slept in my bed
My angel was there, no words to be said

But I saw such great beauty, up there by the throne
Such peace and grandness, more than I had ever known

I saw my brothers, one just a baby so small
The other strong and tan, he stood there so tall

As other family members that had died long before
All hugged and rejoiced, such warm smiles they all bore

The crutches and walkers, they'd used down on earth
Up here were forgotten, they had no more worth

The puppy I'd had as a child, romped and played at our feet
I reached for some fruit, and oh, it tasted so sweet

My parents and sister, all healthy and strong
Joined in the celebration, as we walked with the throng

As we sat and listened, to the God we all knew
I marveled and wondered, that this could be true

The love of my life, his hand did I take
This dream about heaven, how I wished to not awake

My daughters were there, what a race they had run
The pain on earth now forgotten, the agony now done

Heartache was all gone, not a tear was shed
And from my heart cried, the words had to be said

This dream was no longer, but true it would be
Someday I would be there, and really get to see

This gift, this dream, this joy and this pleasure
We can, We can, We can have this dance forever.

www.ingramcontent.com/pod-product-compliance
Lightning Source LLC
Chambersburg PA
CBHW061254040426
42444CB00010B/2379